How To Use This Study Guide

This five-lesson study guide corresponds to *"John's Vision of the Exalted Christ" With Rick Renner* (Renner TV). Each lesson in this study guide covers a topic that is addressed during the program series, with questions and references supplied to draw you deeper into your own private study of the Scriptures on this subject.

To derive the most benefit from this study guide, consider the following:

First, watch or listen to the program prior to working through the corresponding lesson in this guide. (Programs can also be viewed at **renner.org** by clicking on the Media/Archives links or on our Renner Ministries YouTube channel.)

Second, take the time to look up the scriptures included in each lesson. Prayerfully consider their application to your own life.

Third, use a journal or notebook to make note of your answers to each lesson's Study Questions and Practical Application challenges.

Fourth, invest specific time in prayer and in the Word of God to consult with the Holy Spirit. Write down the scriptures or insights He reveals to you.

Finally, take action! Whatever the Lord tells you to do according to His Word, do it.

For added insights on this subject, it is recommended that you obtain Rick Renner's book *A Light in Darkness*. You may also select from Rick's other available resources by placing your order at **renner.org** or by calling 1-800-742-5593.

TOPIC
John on the Isle of Patmos

SCRIPTURES

1. **1 John 5:4** — For whatsoever is born of God overcometh the world: and this is the victory that overcometh the world, even our faith.

2. **Revelation 1:1** — The Revelation of Jesus Christ, which God gave unto him, to shew unto his servants things which must shortly come to pass; and he sent and signified it by his angel unto his servant John.

3. **Revelation 1:4** — John to the seven churches which are in Asia: Grace be unto you, and peace, from him which is, and which was, and which is to come; and from the seven Spirits which are before his throne.

4. **Revelation 1:9** — I John, who also am your brother, and companion in tribulation, and in the kingdom and patience of Jesus Christ, was in the isle that is called Patmos, for the word of God, and for the testimony of Jesus Christ.

GREEK WORDS

1. "revelation" — ἀποκάλυψις (*apokalupsis*): compound of *apo* and *kalupsis*; the word *apo* means away, and the word *kalupsis* describes a veil or a curtain; when compounded, means to remove a veil; to remove a curtain; to have an unobstructed view; a revelation

SYNOPSIS

The five lessons in this study on ***John's Vision of the Exalted Christ*** will focus on the following topics:

- John on the Isle of Patmos
- John Identifies Himself in Revelation 1:9
- How Supernatural Occurrences Take Place
- Why Christ Likens the Church to Candlesticks
- John's Vision of the Exalted Christ

A Note From Rick Renner

I am on a personal quest to see a "revival of the Bible" so people can establish their lives on a firm foundation that will stand strong and endure the test as end-time storm winds begin to intensify.

In order to experience a revival of the Bible in your personal life, it is important to take time each day to read, receive, and apply its truths to your life. James tells us that if we will continue in the perfect law of liberty — refusing to be forgetful hearers, but determined to be doers — we will be blessed in our ways. As you watch or listen to the programs in this series and work through this corresponding study guide, I trust you will search the Scriptures and allow the Holy Spirit to help you hear something new from God's Word that applies specifically to your life. I encourage you to be a doer of the Word He reveals to you. Whatever the cost, I assure you — it will be worth it.

> Thy words were found, and I did eat them;
> and thy word was unto me the joy and rejoicing of mine heart:
> for I am called by thy name, O Lord God of hosts.
> — Jeremiah 15:16

Your brother and friend in Jesus Christ,

Rick Renner

Unless otherwise indicated, all scripture quotations are taken from the *King James Version* of the Bible.

John's Vision of the Exalted Christ

Copyright © 2022 by Rick Renner
1814 W. Tacoma St.
Broken Arrow, OK 74012-1406

Published by Rick Renner Ministries
www.renner.org

ISBN 13: 978-1-6675-0216-8

ISBN 13 eBook: 978-1-6675-0217-5

The emphasis of this lesson:

The word "revelation" means *to remove a curtain or veil*, enabling what was once hidden to be clearly seen. That is what the apostle John experienced on the isle of Patmos. After being supernaturally preserved from certain death, John was sent to Patmos as a political prisoner. It was there that the Holy Spirit pulled back the curtain and allowed him to see Jesus as he had never seen Him before.

In First John 5:4, the apostle John wrote a verse that today is known as a powerful statement of faith. He said, "For whatsoever is born of God overcometh the world: and this is the victory that overcometh the world, even our faith." The word "world" here is the word *kosmos*, which describes *the organized systems of society*. Essentially, this passage tells us that as believers, we have a faith that overcomes and overrides the world's system. It doesn't matter what life or the enemy tries to throw at us, the person who is moving in faith has the victory and overcomes the world's system.

Now, you may have heard this verse before, but what you may not know is what John had gone through before he wrote it. When you understand the death-inducing conditions he endured, this passage takes on a whole new meaning. When John wrote this verse, he was not just giving us a theological statement. He was talking about what faith had done in his own life, which is what we are going to clearly see in this lesson.

The Meaning of the Word 'Revelation'

Let's begin our study with Revelation 1:1, which says, "The Revelation of Jesus Christ, which God gave unto him, to shew unto his servants things which must shortly come to pass; and he sent and signified it by his angel unto his servant John." In this verse, we see the word "revelation," which is the Greek word *apokalupis*, a very important word in the New Testament. It is a compound of the words *apo*, which means *away*, and the word *kalupsis*, which describes *a veil* or *a curtain*. When these words are compounded, the new word *apokalupis* means *to remove a veil* or *to remove a curtain; to have an unobstructed view; a revelation*.

If a curtain is closed, you can't see what's on the other side. There is something on the other side, but the view is obstructed. You simply don't have the ability to see what is behind it. When this word *kalupsis* (*veil* or *curtain*) is compounded with the word *apo* — which means *away* — it depicts *the sudden removal of the veil or curtain*. It's as if someone pulls on the cord of a curtain, and the curtain begins to open up. At first, just a little can be seen, and then a little more and a little more until the curtain or veil is completely removed. The wider and wider the curtain pulls apart, the clearer and clearer your view becomes. That is what it means to have a "revelation" (*apokalupis*), and it is what John experienced while living on the isle of Patmos.

When the Holy Spirit personally gives you a revelation about something, He pulls back the spiritual curtain and allows you to personally see something about God, yourself, or a situation that you were unable to see on your own. In John's case, the revelation he received was an unveiling of who Jesus really is. What previously had obstructed his understanding and perception of Christ was removed, and the true picture of who He is came into clear view. The Holy Spirit pulled back the curtain and enabled John to see Jesus like he had never seen Him before. This was not a "new Christ." It is the same Christ He has always been, only now the hindrance was removed.

Why John Repeatedly Identified Himself

In Revelation 1, it is noted three times in nine verses that *John* is the one who was communicating the revelation. Verses one, four, and nine include this emphasis. In fact, in verse 9, it says "I John, who also am your brother, and companion in tribulation, and in the kingdom and patience of Jesus Christ, was in the isle that is called Patmos, for the word of God, and for the testimony of Jesus Christ" (Revelation 1:9).

This opening phrase, "I John," inserts the Greek word *ego* — meaning "I"). This word indicates that John was emphatically drawing attention to himself. It is as if he was screaming to his readers, "Hey, it's me — John. It's really me!" This is important for the reason that many believers across the Roman Empire were suffering for their faith, and they desperately needed encouragement.

History reveals that at that moment in time, John was the last living survivor of the original 12 apostles. All the others had been martyred for their faith. Therefore, his letter to believers carried great weight and authority. When Christians heard that John was still alive, it was great news. Again and again, John confirmed, "It's me! It's really me — John. If you've wondered if I was still alive, I am still here!"

IMPORTANT CHURCH HISTORY FROM EARLY CHRISTIAN WRITERS

The Apostle John Took Care of Mary After Jesus' Crucifixion

The book of Acts tells us that the apostles were scattered in the early days of the Church as a result of persecution, and according to Church history, most of the apostles were no longer living in Jerusalem. Although they did return for meetings from time to time, they had relocated to other places. When the apostle John left Jerusalem, he took Mary, the mother of Jesus, with him.

If you remember, just before Jesus breathed His last breath on the Cross, He looked down at Mary and at John and entrusted His mother's care into John's hands (*see* John 19:26,27). From that moment on, John took Mary into his home and cared for her for the rest of her life. Wherever he went, she went. When John relocated to the region of Asia, Mary went with him.

Timothy Served As the Pastor of the Church of Ephesus

We know that during the earlier years of the church of Ephesus, Timothy was the pastor. Paul had taken him under his wing and mentored him like a spiritual son for many years. When persecution increased against the Church after the Great Fire of Rome, it seems that Timothy began to fight against a spirit of fear. That is when Paul wrote to him and said, "For God hath not given us the spirit of fear; but of power, and of love, and of a sound mind" (2 Timothy 1:7).

By God's grace, Timothy matured and gained victory over fear and became a strong church leader. In fact, church history documents that Timothy was the pastor of Ephesus until he was 80 years old. According to Early Church writings, it was at that time that a pagan parade was being held on Curetes Street, which ran through the heart of Ephesus. Sometime during that parade, Timothy came out of his house and began boldly rebuking the pagan participants for their ungodly acts. Enraged by Timothy's accusations, the pagans struck him down and killed him right in the middle of Curetes Street. Thus, he died courageously in faith at the age of 80.

John Became Overseer in Asia
After Paul's Death

For the first few years after John went to Asia, Paul was the leading apostle presiding over all the churches in the region. He had a tremendous impact in the lives of people in that area all the way up to the year 67 AD when he was executed for his faith. History tells us that there was a great fire in Rome in 64 AD, which was more than likely started by Nero's henchmen. It seems Nero wanted to build a new palace in a particular section of the city, and when the senate wouldn't let him, he sent his minions to set the buildings on fire in the area where he wanted to erect his new home.

Nero needed to pin the blame on someone, so he claimed the Christians did it — and said Paul was one of the chief arsonists behind it. These false accusations by Nero launched a deadly wave of persecution against the Church in Rome, as well as in all the larger cities of the Roman Empire. Ephesus was one of those cities. Paul had planted a church in that pagan city, and it had grown into one of the biggest, most influential churches in Asia. In fact, the church of Ephesus was the ministry center where church leaders were raised up and trained and sent out to minister in other cities.

After Paul was falsely accused as a chief arsonist, he was executed in 67 AD. He was killed as a criminal for a crime he didn't commit. Soon after Paul's death, John became the presiding bishop over all the churches in the region of Asia. Since he had already relocated to Ephesus and was ministering in Asia, the transition into his new leadership role was virtually seamless.

John Lived on a Hilltop in Ephesus
Above the Temple of Artemis

Now, Early Church records tell us John lived on a hilltop just above and behind the Temple of Artemis. It was Polycrates, the bishop of Ephesus, who lived about 30 years after John's death, who identified the place where John lived. To be clear, the Temple of Artemis was one of the most wicked sites on the planet, housing about 6,000 priests and priestesses who were continually offering sacrifices to demon gods inside. This place was so huge that it was listed as one of the seven wonders of the ancient world. No location was more horrific than this temple, and John lived just a stone's throw from it. In fact, from his hilltop home, he could see the smoke billowing into the air from the sacrifices made to Artemis.

As an apostle and a bishop, John had to meet with many church leaders who came to see him from all parts of Asia and the Roman Empire. Because he lived outside the city limits, the police and the authorities basically left him alone. If he had lived in the city of Ephesus itself, he would have had many problems doing ministry. First, it would have been very troublesome for church leaders because of political persecution. Second, Domitian was ruler of Rome at the time, and he was strongly against the Christian faith. After he declared himself to be lord and god, he required the entire Empire to worship him. It was for this reason that the church of Ephesus and Timothy were having so many problems.

Thus, John's very remote location — a rural place on the hill just above the Temple of Artemis where no one would think to find an apostle or a bishop — was divinely strategic. It was from this hilltop home that John took care of Mary, the mother of Jesus, until the time of her death. After her passing, he continued to live in this same place and provide guidance to the churches for about 30 years as the apostle and bishop — the *episkopos* — of Asia Minor. Again, he accepted this role in the year 67 AD, taking the place of the apostle Paul after his death.

John Was Arrested and Sentenced To Die

According to church history, John was arrested at the age of 92 or 93, and we believe his arrest came because he refused to burn incense to a statue of Domitian. Domitian had declared empire-wide that he was lord and god and required everyone everywhere to worship him, and part of that required worship was burning incense to his image. Before you walked into a market to shop, you had to burn a pinch of incense. Likewise, before you could enter the next region of the city, you had to burn a pinch of incense. It is likely that at some point when John came into the city of Ephesus, he passed one of these statues and refused to burn incense. When someone in authority saw that John didn't pay homage, police were dispatched to his house to arrest him.

Swiftly, John was brought by ship to the city of Rome where he was to stand trial before Emperor Domitian himself. The reason Domitian required John, an elderly man, to come to Rome was because John was the last living apostle of Jesus Christ, and when Domitian heard he was still alive, he wanted to see him personally. When John finally stood in front of Domitian, the Emperor demanded he reject his faith and worship him. Of course, John refused because he was a devoted servant of Jesus Christ, so Domitian sentenced him to death.

Many Early Christian writers, such as Tertullian, tell us that John was thrown into a vat of boiling oil. Although this sounds rather bizarre to us, this was a method of persecution and torture that was regularly used by the Romans, and it was often done when they wanted to create a horrific death for someone. Thus, John was bound and thrown into the boiling oil. Normally, the oil was so hot that it would have cooked the victim quickly and caused his flesh to fall off the bones. In John's case, when the executioners dragged the flesh hook through the oil, instead of bringing up the skeletal remains, Early Christian writers tell us John came out of the oil completely unscathed — he was sustained by the power of God!

When Domitian saw that John was alive and unharmed, he was terrified. "Take this man and get him out of my sight!" he demanded. "Exile him to Patmos." So John, who was in his early 90s and had just been placed in boiling oil and supernaturally preserved, was now being sent back to Ephesus where he was put on a ship and deposited on the isle of Patmos. What is interesting is that Patmos was 60 miles from Ephesus and 24 miles off the coast of what is today modern Turkey. But those 60 miles must have seemed like thousands.

After Being Supernaturally Saved From Death, John Was Imprisoned on the Isle of Patmos

Make no mistake: Patmos was a horrible place. It had been occupied by several previous civilizations, and they had stripped it of all of its vegetation, utilizing all its trees for timber. There was nothing left on Patmos but rocks and an ancient temple to the goddess Artemis on the island's highest peak.

The prisoners sent to Patmos fell into one of two categories: those considered *regular* criminals and those considered *political* prisoners. As a rule, regular criminals were treated worse, but if you were a political prisoner, you were treated with a degree of respect. When John was sent to the isle of Patmos, he was placed there as a political prisoner. Consequently, he was allowed to roam the island like other political prisoners. But that was the extent of his benefits. As a political prisoner, he was given no clothes, no water, and no food. He had to fend for himself. Hence, he wandered the island daily, looking to meet his basic needs.

One thing we know from historical sources is that when John went to Patmos, he was accompanied by a man named Prochorus who served as his secretary. He was actually one of the very first deacons elected to serve at the church in Jerusalem when the Church was birthed (*see* Acts 6:1-6). In those days, it was common for notable individuals to travel with assistants or secretaries. So when John and Prochorus arrived, they quickly began to look for a place to live. Before long, they found and moved into a cave, which happened to be located just below another Temple of Artemis. It was as if John couldn't get away from this pagan goddess.

In any case, it was in that cave on Patmos — the "Cave of the Revelation" as it is called today —that John received the Revelation of Jesus Christ. One day unexpectedly, Jesus stepped inside the cave and gave John a revelation of Himself. Suddenly, the curtains were pulled back, and John saw into the realm of the spirit and caught a glimpse of Christ that he had never seen before, and what he saw is what we now know as the book of Revelation.

What's also interesting is that Early Christian writers tell us there were so many political prisoners exiled to Patmos that they actually formed communities. It seems that entire families were exiled there, and by the time John arrived on Patmos there were a number of these small prison communities in place. John wasted no time before he began to evangelize these groups. In fact, it's very well documented that John established several local churches on Patmos, igniting a thriving faith community in the very short time he was there.

Historical sources from the period tell us John was on Patmos until the death of Domitian in the year 96 AD. After Domitian died, amnesty was given to political prisoners, which enabled John to receive his freedom. Hence, after 18 months of being imprisoned on Patmos with his servant Prochorus — scavenging to provide their own water, food, and clothing — John was released. He was then placed on a ship and carried from Patmos back to the city of Ephesus where he moved into his hilltop home just above and behind the Temple of Artemis. Now an elderly man in his mid-90s, John continued his apostolic ministry, overseeing the churches of

Asia. It was from that same home, he wrote the gospel of John, as well as First, Second, and Third John.

So when John wrote First John 5:4 and said, "For whatsoever is born of God overcometh the world: and this is the victory that overcometh the world, even our faith," he wasn't just speaking some theological-sounding rhetoric. He was actually speaking from his personal experience that he had walked through. He had a testimony in which he could personally declare that *faith* is our victory that overcomes the world. And in the same way, your God-given measure of faith will overcome anything you're facing!

STUDY QUESTIONS

Study to shew thyself approved unto God, a workman that needeth not to be ashamed, rightly dividing the word of truth.
— 2 Timothy 2:15

1. What new historical facts did you learn in this lesson about Paul, Timothy, and the apostle John? What stood out to you about his time in Ephesus and his imprisonment on Patmos?

2. Remember how John shared that our faith is the victory that enables us to overcome the world? What do you think that might look like in *your* life? How is our faith released to help us overcome? (*Hint*: Check out Hebrews 11 and Revelation 12:11.)

3. The way God rescued John from death at the emperor's hands is truly miraculous and a clear expression of His magnificent power. Can you recall anyone else in Scripture who found themselves sentenced to death for choosing not to worship a ruler? (Consider Daniel 3 and 6:10-24.) How do these stories parallel John's?

PRACTICAL APPLICATION

But be ye doers of the word, and not hearers only, deceiving your own selves.
— James 1:22

1. Think back to the original meaning of the word "revelation." Has God ever "pulled back the curtain" to reveal something to you, maybe about Him, about yourself, or about a situation you were going through?

What did you learn? How is that revelation still equipping you in your walk with Him today?

2. After John's release from Patmos, he was living just a stone's throw from the active temple of Artemis, which was filled with thousands of priests and priestesses making sacrifices constantly. Can you imagine what it was like to literally live in the presence of so much evil? In the same way, we live in a world that is becoming increasingly depraved every day. How did Jesus and Paul say we should live in the middle of so much darkness (*see* Matthew 5:13-16 and Ephesians 5:1-20)? What is the Holy Spirit saying to you about the way you do life?

LESSON 2

TOPIC

John Identifies Himself in Revelation 1:9

SCRIPTURES

1. **Revelation 1:1** — The Revelation of Jesus Christ, which God gave unto him, to shew unto his servants things which must shortly come to pass; and he sent and signified it by his angel unto his servant John.

2. **Revelation 1:4** — John to the seven churches which are in Asia: Grace be unto you, and peace, from him which is, and which was, and which is to come; and from the seven Spirits which are before his throne.

3. **Revelation 1:9-11** — I John, who also am your brother, and companion in tribulation, and in the kingdom and patience of Jesus Christ, was in the isle that is called Patmos, for the word of God, and for the testimony of Jesus Christ. I was in the Spirit on the Lord's day, and heard behind me a great voice, as of a trumpet, saying, I am Alpha and Omega, the first and the last: and, What thou seest, write in a book, and send it unto the seven churches which are in Asia; unto Ephesus, and unto Smyrna, and unto Pergamos, and unto Thyatira, and unto Sardis, and unto Philadelphia, and unto Laodicea.

4. **Acts 10:10** — And he became very hungry, and would have eaten: but while they made ready, he fell into a trance.

GREEK WORDS

1. "revelation" — ἀποκάλυψις (*apokalupsis*): compound of *apo* and *kalupsis*; the word *apo* means away, and the word *kalupsis* describes a veil or a curtain; when compounded, means to remove a veil; to remove a curtain; to have an unobstructed view; a revelation

2. "brother" — ἀδελφός (*adelphos*): a medical term to describe the womb of a woman; one born out of the same womb; a brother; a military term to denote a fellow comrade

3. "companion" — συγκοινωνός (*sugkoinonos/sunkoinonos*): compound of *sun* and *koinonos*; the word *sun* means two of us or joint partners, and the word *koinonos* means to share something in common or to have a common experience; compounded, pictures a companion; a joint partner; two or more who share the same experience

4. "tribulation" — θλῖψις (*thlipsis*): a heavy pressure situation; to be pinned against the wall; a crushing situation; a debilitating situation; to feel suffocated by events

5. "kingdom" — βασιλεία (*basileia*): kingdom; the rule of God; the kingdom of God

6. "patience" — ὑπομονή (*hupomone*): patience; endurance; one who doesn't budge, flinch, or move for any reason; "hang-in-there" power; the attitude that holds out, holds on, outlasts, perseveres, and hangs in there, never giving up, refusing to surrender to obstacles, and turning down every opportunity to quit

7. "was" — γίνομαι (*ginomai*): something that takes one off guard or by surprise

8. "fell into" — γίνομαι (*ginomai*): something that takes one off guard or by surprise

9. "spirit" — ἐν πνεύματι (*en pneumati*): in spirit; a spiritual dimension

10. "Lord's day" — κυριακός (*kuriakos*): by the end of the First Century, it typically denoted the imperial day of the emperor; a day to worship the emperor; a significant function in the imperial cult of the emperor

SYNOPSIS

The last book of the Bible is called "Revelation." It is not, as some have mistakenly called it, the book of Revelations. There is no "s" at the end; it is simply the book of Revelation, and it is a written record of the apostle John's Revelation of Jesus Christ.

In Revelation 1:1, John wrote, "**The Revelation of Jesus Christ**, which God gave unto him, to shew unto his servants things which must shortly come to pass; and he sent and signified it by his angel unto his servant John." The word "revelation" here is the Greek word *apokalupis*, which is a compound of the words *apo* and *kalupsis*. The word *apo* means *away*, and the word *kalupsis*, describes *a veil* or *a curtain*. When these words are joined to form *apokalupis*, it means *to remove a veil* or *to remove a curtain*; *to have an unobstructed view*.

Imagine you're sitting in a theater, and there is a huge red curtain running from one side of the stage to the other. You can't see anything behind the thick red velvet, but once the director gives the signal, the curtains are quickly pulled back, revealing to you what was on the other side all along. What was once *hidden* is now *clearly seen* because the curtain has been *removed*. That is what this word "revelation" (*apokalupis*) means.

Therefore, when John talks about, "The Revelation of Jesus Christ, which God gave unto him… (Revelation 1:1)," he is talking about how the Holy Spirit supernaturally removed the veil and allowed him to see Jesus in His exalted state. What previously had obstructed his understanding and perception of Jesus was removed, and the true picture of who He is came into clear view.

Remember, John had walked and talked with Jesus for years, and he carried many fond memories of doing life with Him. He vividly remembered the sound of His voice, the magnetism of His eyes, and being together with Him on countless occasions (*see* 1 John 1:1). But when the Holy Spirit revealed Jesus to John on the isle of Patmos, John saw Jesus as he had never seen Him before. Jesus' human image was superseded by His glorified, kingly image, and John recorded it for all who would believe.

The emphasis of this lesson:

John was the last living apostle who became the overseer of all the churches in Asia after Paul's death. He called himself the *brother* and

companion in tribulation of his readers, suffering for the Kingdom of God and the testimony of Jesus. It was during one of the darkest moments of his life that he unexpectedly received the Revelation of Christ.

John — the Last Living Apostle

In the first nine verses of Revelation, the name "John" appears three times. In verse 1, it says, "his servant *John*." In verse 4, it says, "*John* to the seven churches which are in Asia...." And when we come to verse 9, it begins with the words "I John." The word "I" here is the Greek word *ego*, and John uses this word to emphatically draw attention to himself. It's as if he was screaming to his readers, "Hey, it's me — it's really me, John. Just in case you're wondering who's writing to you, it's John!"

This was very important because many believers across the Roman Empire were suffering for their faith. The Emperor, Domitian, had declared himself to be lord and god, requiring everyone in the Roman Empire to worship him and burn incense to his image. Those who failed to obey this edict were persecuted. At that point in history, all the other original apostles of Jesus had been martyred for their faith, so John was the last living apostle. Therefore, his letter to believers carried great weight and authority. When Christians heard that the apostle John was still alive, it was great news.

Remember, John himself had suffered at the hands of Domitian, more than likely for refusing to burn incense to one of Domitian's statues. After a failed attempt at boiling John in oil, Domitian banished him to the isle of Patmos where he lived in exile for 18 months as a political prisoner with his assistant Prochorus. During that time, no one in the Church heard from John, and many likely thought that he had died. Therefore, when John wrote Revelation and identified himself as still being alive, it must have ignited a spark of hope and confidence in the weary saints.

If you think about it, John could have written and identified himself as "the illustrious disciple of Jesus" or "the last living apostle" or "the disciple hand-picked by Jesus to care for Mary, His mother." But John refrained from all such boasting and instead, with great maturity of character, he referred to himself as, "I John, who also am your brother..." (Revelation 1:9).

We Are 'Brothers,'
Born From the Womb of God

When John called himself the "brother" of his readers, he used the Greek word *adelphos*, which is derived from the word *delphos*, the medical term describing *the womb of a woman*. When the letter "a" is attached to the front, it changes the meaning. The new word — *adelphos* — describes *two or more who were born from the same womb*. John's use of this word was the equivalent of him telling his readers, "You and I are 'brothers' (*adelphos*) — we are born from the same womb of humanity. We have the same struggles, the same emotions, the same victories, and the same defeats. We're also 'brothers' (*adelphos*) because we are born from the same womb of God."

What's interesting about this word *adelphos*, translated "brother," is that it was later used in a military sense to depict *brothers in battle, a comrade*; or *a brotherhood*. It was first popularized by Alexander the Great, who was viewed as one of the greatest soldiers in human history. Every Greek soldier wanted to be affiliated with Alexander. So every now and then, Alexander would host a huge award ceremony and call especially brave soldiers up on stage to stand with him. He'd wrap his arm around each soldier and say to all the adoring onlookers, "Let everyone in the empire know that Alexander is proud to be the brother (*adelphos*) of this soldier!" It was his way of saying, "Brother, you and I are in this fight together!" Hence, the word *adelphos* carried the idea of *camaraderie* and was the greatest honor that could be conferred upon a soldier.

By using the word "brother" (*adelphos*), John placed himself down in the trenches with the believers who were really suffering and struggling in their faith. This term of endearment was John's way of saying, "I'm so proud to be your brother! You're still in the fight, you're still slugging it out, and you're still going for the victory. I'm honored to be connected with you — my comrade in the Lord." These words of praise and honor from the apostle John must have been a great boost in the morale of all his readers.

'Companions in Tribulation'

In addition to identifying himself as "brother" to his readers, John also called himself a "companion in tribulation" (Revelation 1:9). The word "companion" here is the Greek word *sugkoinonos (sunkoinonos)*, a compound of the words *sun* and *koinonos*. The word *sun* means *two of us* or *joint partners*, and the word *koinonos* means *to share something in common* or *to have a common experience*. When these words are compounded, the new word *sugkoinonos* pictures *a companion, a joint partner*, or *two or more who share the same experience*.

By using this word, John is telling his readers, "The difficulties you're experiencing are not unique to you. Believers everywhere are suffering, including me. I'm a joint partner in tribulation." The word "tribulation" here is the Greek word *thlipsis*, and it describes *a heavy pressure situation; a crushing situation*; or *a debilitating situation*. It carries the idea of *being pinned against the wall* or *feeling suffocated by events*. The apostle Paul used this word in Second Corinthians 1:8 when he said that he and his companions were "pressed out of measure."

When John said he was a "companion in tribulation" (Revelation 1:9), he was saying, "What I've been through has been devastating, debilitating, and crushing. There were times when I felt suffocated and didn't know if I would be able to breathe my next breath." John is *not* saying these things to one-up his readers or gain their pity; he's speaking to his flock as a pastor who has also gone through extremely tough situations. Indeed, being boiled in oil and exiled to the isle of Patmos were definitely not walks in the park.

John Stood for God's Kingdom in the Supernatural Endurance of Jesus

Through it all, John never lost sight of the reason he was suffering. He said it was for "…the kingdom and patience of Jesus Christ…" (Revelation 1:9). The word "kingdom" here is the Greek word *basileia*, which means *kingdom* and describes *the rule of God* or *the kingdom of God*. It is so vital to remember that God can use all the battles and hardships we face to help others come to Christ and grow in relationship with Him. That's what it means to advance the kingdom of God.

John basically declared, "I stand for God's kingdom rule, and as a result I am experiencing the *patience* of Jesus Christ." In Greek, the word "patience" is *hupomone*. It is a compound of the word *hupo*, meaning *to be under*, and the word *meno*, which means *"I abide"* or *"I stay."* When compounded, the word *hupomone* is really a picture of *endurance*. It depicts *one who is staying in his place (meno) and is under a heavy load (hupo)*.

Thus, "patience" (*hupomone*) is *staying power* or *hang-in-there power*. It is *the attitude that holds out, holds on, outlasts, perseveres, and hangs in there, never giving up, refusing to surrender to obstacles, and turning down every opportunity to quit.* It pictures *one under a heavy load, but who refuses to bend, break, or surrender because he is convinced that the territory, promise, or principle under assault rightfully belongs to him.* A better translation of the word "patience" would be *endurance, stamina, or durability.*

So when the apostle John said he was experiencing the "patience" of Jesus, he was saying, "I don't care what Emperor Domitian does to me or if I'm stuck living in a cave on this wretched island. I've made up my mind I'm not budging, I'm not flinching, I'm not going to quit or surrender! I'm going to stay firm in my commitment to Jesus." This is a picture of "patience" (*hupomone*). John had been given this supernatural enduring power of Christ, and it was enabling him to remain faithful to God even in the midst of life-threatening pressure. And this same grace that God gave John is the same grace He has for you today.

Friend, please don't believe the lie that you're alone in your pain — countless brothers and sisters in Christ are dealing with extreme difficulties as well. We are each other's *comrades* in battle and *companions in tribulation.* What we're doing is for the Kingdom of God and the rescue of people's souls for eternity. When you make a decision to remain committed to what Christ has called you to do — not budging, not flinching, and not surrendering — God will cultivate in you the faith that overcomes and overrides the world's system, just like He did for John (*see* 1 John 5:4).

The Revelation of Jesus Was Totally Unexpected and Unanticipated

John went on to say, "…[I] was in the isle that is called Patmos, for the word of God, and for the testimony of Jesus Christ" (Revelation 1:9). Interestingly, the word "was" here is quite significant. It is the Greek word *ginomai*, and it always describes *something that takes you off guard or by surprise.* It depicts *a transition from one realm to another.* By using this word, John was saying, "Through a strange set of circumstances that I didn't expect and I cannot explain, I somehow (*ginomai*) found myself banished from society, living in a cave on a remote island, and scavenging daily for food and water. I could have never predicted the pressuring series of events that brought me here."

Remember, John had been sent to the isle of Patmos by Emperor Domitian after he miraculously survived being dropped in boiling oil. Although he had the status of a political prisoner and was free to roam the island, he still had to find water, food, and clothing for himself. The reason for John's exile is made clear in Revelation 1:9: "…for the testimony of Jesus Christ," so it was not about John personally, but about who and what John stood for.

In Revelation 1:10, John went on to say, "I was in the Spirit on the Lord's day, and heard behind me a great voice, as of a trumpet." In this verse, John begins to tell us how he received the book of Revelation. First, notice the word "was." It is once again the word *ginomai*, which always describes *something that takes you off guard or by surprise.* John's use of this word here tells us that receiving the Revelation of Jesus was totally unexpected and took him off guard.

A great example of this word *ginomai* is found in Act 10:10 where it says that Peter "…became very hungry, and would have eaten: but while they made ready, he fell into a trance." The phrase "fell into" here is the Greek word *ginomai*, which again is *something that takes one off guard or by surprise.* This tells us that while Peter was up on the rooftop waiting for lunch, he was not anticipating falling into a trance — entering into another dimension took him completely off guard. That same kind of unexpected, surprising turn of events is what the apostle John experienced on the isle of Patmos.

It Happened 'on the Lord's Day'

When did this unforeseen revelation take place? He said, "I was in the Spirit on the Lord's day…" (Revelation 1:10). In the *King James Version*, the word Spirit is capitalized, but in the original text, it is lowercase. This word "spirit" is a translation of the Greek words *en pneumati*, which means *in spirit*. In other words, John is saying he entered *a spiritual dimension*.

What's interesting is that John said it happened "on the Lord's day." At first glance, you might think he is referring to Saturday, which would be the Jewish Sabbath, or possibly Sunday, the day Christians celebrate Jesus' resurrection. However, it is neither of those days. The phrase "Lord's day" in Greek is *kuriakos*, which was a technical term coined by Emperor Domitian toward the end of the First Century to denote *the imperial day of the emperor.* This was a day set aside monthly to worship the emperor — a significant ritual in the imperial cult of the emperor.

So what John's telling us is that on the day when the rest of the Roman world was worshiping the demented and depraved Emperor Domitian who claimed to be god, John was suddenly and unexpectedly swept away into another dimension — a dimension of the spirit realm. It was in that divine moment the Commander-in-Chief and Head of the armies of Heaven, the Son of the Living God, stepped into the cave with John and revealed Himself like never before.

John then added, "…[I] heard behind me a great voice, as of a trumpet, saying, I am Alpha and Omega, the first and the last: and, What thou seest, write in a book, and send it unto the seven churches which are in Asia; unto Ephesus, and unto Smyrna, and unto Pergamos, and unto Thyatira, and unto Sardis, and unto Philadelphia, and unto Laodicea" (Revelation 1:10,11). What a commission!

What does Jesus mean when He identifies Himself as the "Alpha and Omega, the first and the last"? And what do the first and last letters of the Hebrew alphabet have to do with Christ? We'll answer these questions and explore how supernatural events like this take place in our next lesson.

STUDY QUESTIONS

**Study to shew thyself approved unto God, a workman that
needeth not to be ashamed, rightly dividing the word of truth.
— 2 Timothy 2:15**

1. Do you ever feel like the temptations and tests you're facing are so hard and unusual that no one else can relate to them or understand your situation? How do these passages from God's Word give you hope that there are other believers who are going through — or have been through — what you're experiencing? (*See* First Corinthians 10:13; Second Corinthians 1:5-10; First Peter 5:8-10.)

2. Remember the Greek words for "brother" and "companion"? They create a picture of someone who is truly like a *brother* or *sister* in the battles of life. Whose friendship in Scripture does this make you think of? (Consider First Samuel 18:1-5.) What do you think it might look like to be or have a friend like this?

PRACTICAL APPLICATION

But be ye doers of the word, and not hearers only,
deceiving your own selves.
— James 1:22

1. When John wrote to his readers, he referred to himself as, "I John, who also am your brother..." (Revelation 1:9). A mark of real spiritual maturity — and security in our identity in Christ — is not having to prove how great we are or boast about our accomplishments. What do Paul's words in Philippians 3:1-14 say to you about where our focus should be instead?

2. John was imprisoned in his early 90s on the isle of Patmos and left to scavenge for water and food daily. Yet it was in this dark moment of his life that Jesus showed up and revealed Himself in an unforgettable way. Where are you in your own life right now? Do you feel abandoned or left to survive on your own, like John was? What's one aspect of Jesus' character that you really want or need to be revealed to you right now?

3. Take some time to share how you're feeling with Him, and invite the Holy Spirit to *reveal* Jesus to you more clearly than you've ever seen Him before. Journal anything He shows you or tells you.

4. (Note: this doesn't have to be anything highly detailed or polished — just write or record in some way whatever you hear/see as the Holy Spirit starts speaking to you. It will be a powerful tool for you later on in your walk with God!)

TOPIC

How Supernatural Occurrences Take Place

SCRIPTURES

1. **Revelation 1:1** — The Revelation of Jesus Christ, which God gave unto him, to shew unto his servants things which must shortly come to pass; and he sent and signified it by his angel unto his servant John.

2. **Revelation 1:4** — John to the seven churches which are in Asia: Grace be unto you, and peace, from him which is, and which was, and which is to come; and from the seven Spirits which are before his throne.

3. **Revelation 1:9-13** — I John, who also am your brother, and companion in tribulation, and in the kingdom and patience of Jesus Christ, was in the isle that is called Patmos, for the word of God, and for the testimony of Jesus Christ. I was in the Spirit on the Lord's day, and heard behind me a great voice, as of a trumpet, saying, I am Alpha and Omega, the first and the last: and, What thou seest, write in a book, and send it unto the seven churches which are in Asia; unto Ephesus, and unto Smyrna, and unto Pergamos, and unto Thyatira, and unto Sardis, and unto Philadelphia, and unto Laodicea. And I turned to see the voice that spake with me. And being turned, I saw seven golden candlesticks; And in the midst of the seven candlesticks one like unto the Son of man, clothed with a garment down to the foot, and girt about the paps with a golden girdle.

4. **Acts 10:10** — And he became very hungry, and would have eaten: but while they made ready, he fell into a trance.

5. **Revelation 1:20** — The mystery of the seven stars which thou sawest in my right hand, and the seven golden candlesticks. The seven stars are the angels of the seven churches: and the seven candlesticks which thou sawest are the seven churches.

GREEK WORDS

1. "spirit" — ἐν πνεύματι (*en pneumati*): in spirit; a spiritual dimension
2. "was" — γίνομαι (*ginomai*): something that takes one off guard or by surprise
3. "Lord's day" — κυριακός (*kuriakos*): by the end of the First Century, it typically denoted the imperial day of the emperor; a day to worship the emperor; a significant function in the imperial cult of the emperor
4. "fell into" — γίνομαι (*ginomai*): something that takes one off guard or by surprise
5. "Alpha and Omega" — the Beginning and the End, and everything in between; the All-Sufficient One; everything there is
6. "candlesticks" — λυχνία (*luchnia*): an oil-burning lamp carried by hand, positioned on a table or elevated on a stand; such lamps were fashioned of earthen clay with a reservoir to hold oil and a wick that gave light in darkness once it was lighted; oil-burning lamps were vital to life because they were the only source of light in darkness
7. "gold" — χρυσός (*chrusos*): the most valuable metal or commodity that existed in the ancient world; pure gold
8. "midst" — μέσος (*mesos*): in the very middle; in the very center; to be in the gut or heart of a thing

SYNOPSIS

The Revelation of Jesus Christ is the *unveiling* — the *apokalupsis* — of the glorified person of Jesus Christ. The apostle John was given this unobstructed view of the Lord. Three times in the first nine verses of Chapter 1, John identified himself as the writer of Revelation. It is as if he was shouting to his readers, "Hey, it's me — it's really me, John, who is writing to you!" When John's readers realized he was still alive, it gave them hope and encouragement to press on in their faith even in the midst of great persecution.

The emphasis of this lesson:

When you study how dreams and visions happen in Scripture, they never occur when people are trying to force their way into the spirit realm. Instead, they take place as people are living their lives, going about their business. That's what happened to John on Patmos, and what he received from Jesus, he was told to share with the seven major churches in Asia, which were like pure gold in Jesus' eyes.

John Was Imprisoned on Patmos

In Revelation 1:9, John wrote, "I John, who also am your brother, and companion in tribulation, and in the kingdom and patience of Jesus Christ, was in the isle that is called Patmos, for the word of God, and for the testimony of Jesus Christ." In the last two lessons, we learned that Patmos was one of the most foreboding places on the planet at that time. Like a modern-day Alcatraz, Patmos was a repository for criminals of all sorts — particularly common criminals and political offenders.

It seems John had been arrested in the city of Ephesus for some type of political crime. In Ephesus, there was a massive square called Domitian Square, and in that square, there was an enormous temple to Emperor Domitian where about 6,000 priests and priestesses served him. There was also a huge statue of Domitian and an altar where sacrifices were offered to him, and people worshiped him as lord and god. Fragments of this statue can be seen today in the museum at Ephesus.

In those days, Ephesus maintained a strong emphasis on the worship of Emperor Domitian. Since John lived in Ephesus, it seems likely that he was caught walking through the city and refusing to bow to Domitian's statue or to burn incense to him. Whatever the case, someone took note of his refusal to pay homage, and John was arrested. After standing trial before Domitian in Rome, he was eventually sent to the isle of Patmos, located about 24 miles from Ephesus. John, who was in his early 90s, had committed no crime, yet was suffering for the Word of God and the testimony of Jesus Christ.

The Revelation He Received Was Unexpected and Took Place 'in the Spirit on the Lord's Day'

Indeed, Patmos was a dark place, and in a moment when John was probably feeling somewhat abandoned, Jesus stepped into his situation. John describes it like this: "I was in the Spirit on the Lord's day, and heard behind me a great voice, as of a trumpet" (Revelation 1:10). It is important to note that the word "spirit" is never capitalized in Greek. Thus, its meaning must be interpreted based on context. In this particular case, it should be lowercased as it doesn't mean, "I was in the Holy Spirit." Rather, John was saying, "I was in the *spirit realm*" or "I was in *a spiritual dimension*."

How John got into the realm of the spirit is found in the meaning of the words "I was," which is a translation of the Greek word *ginomai*. This word always describes *something that takes you off guard* or *something that takes you by surprise*. By using this word, John tells us emphatically that he doesn't know how he got there or how the event took place. It was the last thing he would have anticipated on that particular day, which he identifies as "the Lord's day."

The phrase "Lord's day" is a translation of the Greek word *kuriakos*, which doesn't describe Saturday — the Jewish Sabbath — or Sunday, which became the day of the week when Christians worship. The word *kuriakos* is from the word *kurios*, which means "lord," but in this case, it refers to *"the imperial day of the emperor."* This was a day set aside monthly to worship Emperor Domitian, who had declared himself to be lord and god. On that day everyone in the empire was to make sacrifices to images of Domitian, and they were to consecrate that day as an offering of worship to him.

So on the day when the whole Roman Empire was involved in the worship of Domitian, a false god, the apostle John was in his cave on the isle of Patmos receiving the Revelation of Jesus. Imagine that. As John was going about his daily routine during his days of imprisonment, he had a *ginomai* experience! With this understanding, the beginning of Revelation 1:10 could be translated, "I don't know how it happened, but through a strange series of events, in a way that I could have never predicted, and I could never duplicate, I came to find myself suddenly in the realm of the spirit on the day set aside for the worship of the emperor."

This word *ginomai* is also used in Acts 10:10 to describe how Peter received his vision when he was on the rooftop in Joppa waiting for lunch. The Bible says that Peter "...became very hungry, and would have eaten: but while they made ready, he fell into a trance." The phrase "fell into" here is the Greek word *ginomai*, which again is *something that takes one off guard or by surprise*. This tells us that when Peter was up on the rooftop, he was not waiting for or anticipating falling into a trance. Yet suddenly and unexpectedly, he entered into a spiritual dimension and received a vision from God.

When you study how dreams and visions happen in Scripture, they never occur when people are trying to force their way into the spirit realm. Instead, they take place as people are just living their lives and going about their business. Suddenly, they have a *ginomai* experience when

God literally invades their world and supernaturally reveals something of great importance. That's what we find happening to John in Revelation 1:10 while he's in his cave on the isle of Patmos. When everyone else was worshiping Emperor Domitian on his special day of the month (*kuriakos*), the real Emperor of the Universe stepped into John's cave! It was a sudden, unanticipated, unexpected *ginomai* experience that John didn't plan nor could he ever replicate.

John Heard Jesus' 'Great Voice'

When John was in the realm of the spirit, he said, "...[I] heard behind me a great voice, as of a trumpet" (Revelation 1:10). The word "great" here is the Greek word *mega*, and the word "voice" is the word *phoneo*. When these two words come together, it forms the word *megaphone*, which is where we get the word *megaphone*. This denotes *a very loud, booming voice*, which is what John heard behind him.

When we come to verse 11, we see that the voice was "saying" something. The tense of the Greek word "saying" here means *saying and saying and saying*. It is an announcement being repeated over and over and over. What was the voice of Jesus declaring to John? He said, "...I am Alpha and Omega, the first and the last..." (Revelation 1:11). The word *alpha* is the beginning of the Greek alphabet, and the word *Omega* is the end of it.

What's interesting is that when you find this wording used in Scripture or even in the secular language of that time, it meant, "I am the Beginning and the End, and everything in between. I am the All-Sufficient One; everything there is." Indeed, Jesus is the First and the Last and everything in-between.

Jesus then told John, "...What thou seest, write in a book, and send it unto the seven churches which are in Asia; unto Ephesus, and unto Smyrna, and unto Pergamos [Pergamum], and unto Thyatira, and unto Sardis, and unto Philadelphia, and unto Laodicea" (Revelation 1:11).

Why These Particular Seven Cities and Churches?

Historically, we know Ephesus was the greatest city in all of Asia. In fact, it was one of the largest cities in the Roman Empire. It was in the city of Ephesus that the apostle Paul founded the church of Ephesus in the year 52 AD. After sailing into the harbor of Ephesus, he preached the

Gospel, and the Church was born. It was in Ephesus that Paul's ministry headquarters was established.

Nothing in the plan of God happens by accident, and Ephesus being the first church plant in the region is no exception. Ephesus was called the "gateway to Asia," and it was considered the most illustrious and most intelligent of all the cities. If someone could make it big in Ephesus, then the gateway into the whole of Asia was opened to them. The Holy Spirit sent Paul and his team into Ephesus knowing that if the Gospel could take root in Ephesus, it would open the gateway for the Gospel to permeate into all of Asia. Thus, Paul and his team established the church in Ephesus, and he was there for two years (*see* Acts 19:10).

During Paul's time there, other churches were established. For example, there was a church established in the city of Smyrna, which was just about 35 miles away. Just beyond the city of Smyrna was the city of Pergamum, which was the official seat of the governor or proconsul of Asia. Hence, establishing the Church in the city of Pergamum was a critical achievement. Next, the Church was established in Thyatira, a city that had been built to defend Pergamum. Beyond Thyatira, the Church was established in the city of Sardis — a very wealthy and legendary city. From there, the Church was established in the city of Philadelphia and then in Laodicea. Paul and his team founded churches in all seven of these major cities.

Now sometimes we may wonder, *How is God going to use us and how will He direct us to do His will?* Well, in this particular case, it was very simple. These seven cities were all situated on a single road. It was actually a circular road that was sometimes referred to as the "postal road," and if you began in Ephesus and followed the road, this circular road would eventually take you to all of these cities. Going north from Ephesus brings us to the city of Smyrna, followed by the city of Pergamum. If you keep following the road, you'll run into Thyatira, and just a little further south is the city of Sardis. Keep following the road and it will take you next to Philadelphia and then to the city of Laodicea. If you keep moving west on the same road, it will bring you back to the city of Ephesus.

So when Paul and his team received a divine commandment on how to evangelize Asia, the commandment was very simple: "Follow the road." As they were obedient, the Holy Spirit worked through them to birth the Church in all seven of these major cities.

Who Were the Overseers of These Churches?

Another important bit of history we know is that all seven of these cities became like districts of churches. For example, in the city of Ephesus where Timothy was the first pastor, he was not only the overseer of the church of Ephesus, but also the overseer of all the churches in that region. Likewise, in the city of Smyrna there was a similar situation. There were many churches established in and around that area, and the presiding pastor of Smyrna not only oversaw the church of Smyrna, but also the other churches in the region. This was true for all seven of these cities.

Looking again at Ephesus, we know the apostle Paul started the church there. Before he left, he installed Timothy as the pastor, who served as pastor until he was about 80 years old when he was killed by pagans on Curetes Street in the heart of the city. After Timothy died, the apostle John became the pastor of the church in Ephesus.

How about Smyrna? Looking at a document written in the Second Century, we know that the first pastor there was a man named Stratius. Early Christian writers tell us that Stratius was the natural brother of Timothy. Although Stratius' name is not mentioned in the Bible, in the Second Century, a document was written identifying him — Timothy's brother — as the pastor of the church in Smyrna. Think about it: Timothy was pastoring the church in Ephesus, and his natural brother was pastoring the church in Smyrna. Thus, there was a relationship between these two churches. In fact, there was a relationship between Ephesus and all seven churches because it was from Ephesus that all of these churches had been born.

Now in the middle of this circular road was a place called the Lycus Valley, and in this valley were the cities of Colossae, Hierapolis, and several others where the apostle Paul also ministered and established churches. What is truly remarkable is that Jesus knew that by speaking to each of these seven major churches, He would identify not only the problems they were dealing with but also the issues that every church through all generations would be facing. These seven churches and their particular needs represent the universal needs in all the churches that existed at that time and that will exist throughout the entire Church Age. The fact that there are seven is significant because seven is always a picture of completion.

John 'Turned' To See Who Was Speaking

In Revelation 1:12, John says, "And I turned to see the voice that spake with me...." The phrase "I turned" in Greek literally means *to physically turn around*. The use of this word tells us this was not just a vision; there was an actual physical dimension to what John was experiencing. He literally heard a voice coming from behind him, and when he did, he physically turned to see whose voice was speaking to him.

John continued by saying, "...And being turned, I saw seven golden candlesticks" (Revelation 1:12). Who was it that was speaking to John? It was Jesus. He had already identified Himself in verse 11 when he said, "I'm Alpha and Omega, the first and the last." Thus, this was the voice of Christ Himself who was speaking to John.

It is likely that John recognized the voice because he had heard Jesus speak so many times earlier in his life, and he carried those treasured memories of being with Jesus in his soul for decades, waiting for the moment when he would finally see Jesus again. Therefore, when he heard the familiar voice, the Bible says he physically turned around, and he probably expected to see Jesus.

Much to John's surprise, when he turned around, "...[He] saw seven golden candlesticks" (Revelation 1:12). We know what the candlesticks are because Revelation 1:20 tells us clearly, "...The seven candlesticks which thou sawest are the seven churches." So the seven candlesticks represent each of the seven churches in Ephesus, Smyrna, Pergamum, Thyatira, Sardis, Philadelphia, and Laodicea.

The Significance of the Word 'Candlesticks'

Now, when we hear the word "candlesticks," most of us think of a candle like we use today — a rod-like wax cylinder with a wick running through its center. But that's not the kind of candle being described here. Wax candles like we use today were not widely manufactured until the Fourteenth Century, which is over 1,000 years after the book of Revelation was written.

The word "candlestick" mentioned here in Revelation 1:12 is the Greek word *luchnia*, and it describes *an oil-burning lamp carried by hand, positioned on a table*, or *elevated on a stand*. These First Century lamps were fashioned of earthen clay and had a handle, a reservoir to hold oil, and a spout with a wick that gave light in darkness once it was lighted. Oil-burning lamps like these were vital to life because they were the only source of light in darkness.

What's interesting is that every lamp was different. For example, there were Jewish lamps in the First Century, each with unique decorations that set it apart as Jewish. Then there were Greek lamps, Herodian lamps, and Roman lamps, each with a slightly different shape and a unique design. Although all lamps have the same basic style, structure, and function, they all tend to look a little different. Again, no two lamps were the same, because each one was fashioned by hand.

Similarly, just as no two lamps were exactly alike, no two churches are the same either. Yes, they all have the same basic function and structure. Just as lamps were filled with "oil," churches are filled with the "oil" of the Holy Spirit. Likewise, just as every lamp had a handle, each church has a handle with which they can be carried and directed by the Lord to shine where needed. Furthermore, just as each lamp had a mouth with a wick that was saturated with oil and then lit on fire to give light to everyone in the house, each church is intended to be God's oil lamp in the world. We are to be filled with the precious oil of the Holy Spirit, have a mouth for declaring the Gospel, and when we're saturated with the Holy Spirit and set on fire with the power of God, we become a bright shining lamp to give light in darkness. That is the purpose of the Church.

Why Are the Candlesticks 'Golden'?

As noted, lamps in the First Century were made of clay. They were very fragile, very breakable, but also very replaceable. The strange thing about what John saw is that the seven candlesticks, which represented the seven churches, were not pictured as lamps of clay but as "golden" lamps. This word "golden" is the Greek word *chrusos*, and it describes the *most valuable metal or commodity that existed in the ancient world*. There was nothing more valuable in the First Century than *chrusos* — *pure gold*.

In Jesus' eyes, the Church is like *pure gold*, and He is not ashamed of Her. Even though the Church has defects and problems, in the mind of God and in the eyes of Jesus, the Church is absolutely *golden*. Many people today are familiar with the Church's problems, the defects, and the things they're dissatisfied with. As a result, they tend to shun the Church. But Christ, who is the Head of the Church and gave His Blood to redeem it, is not ashamed of it. In fact, John said Christ is "in the *midst* of the seven candlesticks" (Revelation 1:13). The word "midst" here is the Greek word *mesos*, which means *right in the very middle, the very center, or the very heart or gut of a thing*. That is where Christ is — in the very gut of the Church.

Friend, love *your* church just as Christ loves *the* Church. It doesn't matter what shortcomings you see with your physical eyes. In the mind of Christ and the eyes of God, the Church is like pure gold. It was purchased with the blood of Jesus, and it is precious — it's golden. It is to be filled with the Holy Spirit, and its function is to shine the light in darkness. That's what the Church is for.

STUDY QUESTIONS

Study to shew thyself approved unto God, a workman that needeth not to be ashamed, rightly dividing the word of truth.
— 2 Timothy 2:15

1. What new insights did you learn about each of the seven major cities in Asia — Ephesus, Smyrna, Pergamum, Thyatira, Sardis, Philadelphia, and Laodicea? How were they connected? And why did the Holy Spirit have Paul begin in the city of Ephesus?

2. Prior to this lesson, what did you understand John to mean when he said, "I was in the Spirit on the Lord's day..." (Revelation 1:10)? How does the Greek meaning of the phrases "in the spirit" and "on the Lord's Day" change your understanding of this verse?

PRACTICAL APPLICATION

But be ye doers of the word, and not hearers only, deceiving your own selves.
— James 1:22

1. Just as no two lamps were exactly alike, no two churches are the same, either. Take a few moments to reread the section, "The Significance of the Word 'Candlesticks.'" What is the Holy Spirit showing you about the role of each church — including *your* church — through the vivid imagery of these First Century oil-burning lamps?

2. Many today are aware of the Church's problems and failures, and they're highly frustrated. As a result, they tend to criticize and ridicule

the Church and/or want nothing to do with it. How about you? What's your attitude toward Christ's Church as a whole? Does it make sense that He calls us His Bride? How do you treat its members — especially those who have glaring defects? What does it mean to you to know that the Church is like gold in Jesus' eyes, and He loves Her with His very life? Pray and ask God to help you see people in His Church the way Jesus does.

3. In the Bible, when dreams and visions happen, they never occur when people are trying to force their way into the spirit realm. Instead, they take place as people are living their lives, going about their business. Have you ever had a *ginomai* experience when God suddenly and unexpectedly invaded your world? If so, describe what happened and what He revealed to you? If not, ask the Holy Spirit to open your spiritual eyes to begin seeing things in the realm of the spirit that will bring peace and understanding to your walk with Him. (Consider the example in Second Kings 6:15-18.)

LESSON 4

TOPIC

Why Christ Likens the Church to Candlesticks

SCRIPTURES

1. **Revelation 1:10-16** — I was in the Spirit on the Lord's day, and heard behind me a great voice, as of a trumpet, saying, I am Alpha and Omega, the first and the last: and, What thou seest, write in a book, and send it unto the seven churches which are in Asia; unto Ephesus, and unto Smyrna, and unto Pergamos, and unto Thyatira, and unto Sardis, and unto Philadelphia, and unto Laodicea. And I turned to see the voice that spake with me. And being turned, I saw seven golden candlesticks; And in the midst of the seven candlesticks one like unto the Son of man, clothed with a garment down to the foot, and girt about the paps with a golden girdle. His head and his hairs were white like wool, as white as snow; and his eyes were as a flame of fire; And his feet like unto fine brass, as if they burned in a furnace; and

his voice as the sound of many waters. And he had in his right hand seven stars: and out of his mouth went a sharp twoedged sword: and his countenance was as the sun shineth in his strength.

2. **Revelation 2:1,2** — Unto the angel of the church of Ephesus write; These things saith he that holdeth the seven stars in his right hand, who walketh in the midst of the seven golden candlesticks; I know thy works, and thy labour, and thy patience, and how thou canst not bear them which are evil: and thou hast tried them which say they are apostles, and are not, and hast found them liars.

GREEK WORDS

1. "know" — οἶδα (*oida*): to see or to make a personal observation
2. "works" — ἔργα (*erga*): all of your activities
3. "candlesticks" — λυχνία (*luchnia*): an oil-burning lamp carried by hand, positioned on a table or elevated on a stand; such lamps were fashioned of earthen clay with a reservoir to hold oil and a wick that gave light in darkness once it was lighted; oil-burning lamps were vital to life because they were the only source of light in darkness
4. "gold" — χρυσός (*chrusos*): the most valuable metal or commodity that existed in the ancient world; pure gold
5. "midst" — μέσος (*mesos*): in the very middle; in the very center; to be in the gut or heart of a thing

SYNOPSIS

When John was in the realm of the spirit on the Lord's day, he said he heard a "great voice" (Revelation 1:10). The word "great" here is the Greek word *mega*, and the word "voice" is the word *phoneo*. When these words are compounded, it forms the word *megaphone*, which is where we get the word *megaphone*. This denotes *a very loud, booming voice*, which is what John heard behind him.

In Revelation 1:11, we saw that the voice was "saying" something. The tense of the Greek word "saying" here means *saying and saying and saying*. Over and over again this voice — which was the voice of Jesus — was *conversing* with John declaring, "...I am Alpha and Omega, the first and the last..." (Revelation 1:11). Essentially, what Jesus is saying here is, "I am the Beginning and the End, and everything in between. I am the All-Sufficient One; everything there is."

Jesus then told John, "…What thou seest, write in a book, and send it unto the seven churches which are in Asia; unto Ephesus, and unto Smyrna, and unto Pergamos [Pergamum], and unto Thyatira, and unto Sardis, and unto Philadelphia, and unto Laodicea" (Revelation 1:11). Jesus knew that by speaking to these seven major churches, He would address not only the problems they were facing, but also the issues that every church through all generations would be dealing with. Let's take another look at the significance of each of these cities.

The emphasis of this lesson:

The seven cities Jesus addressed in the book of Revelation were located just a few miles from each other on a circular road, and in each one Paul had planted a church. Jesus knew by personal observation what was going on in each congregation, and He compares the Church to oil-burning lamps. We have the oil of the Spirit, and when we are ignited by God, we shine the light of truth through our lives and the words of our lips.

The Significance of the Seven Cities

The first city was **Ephesus**, which we've noted to be the "gateway to Asia." Once something succeeded in Ephesus, the door was opened for it to go into all of Asia. The Holy Spirit very strategically sent Paul there first because once the Gospel was received and established in Ephesus, it would be free to penetrate the entire continent. In the same way, there are strategic places where God will send you, and while they may not seem particularly important, they are actually door openers for what He has planned ahead.

Second was the city of **Smyrna**, which was just about 35 miles from Ephesus. This was the second place Paul and his team established the Church and where Timothy's brother, Stratius, served as the first pastor. Although his name is not given in Scripture, it does appear in a Second Century document that lists all the pastors in the church of Smyrna. Early Christian writers tell us he was ordained by Paul and was the natural-born, elder brother of Timothy, who was pastoring the church of Ephesus.

Imagine it. Timothy, the younger brother, was pastoring the biggest church in the city of Ephesus, and just up the road was his elder brother pastoring a smaller church in the city of Smyrna. Was there competition or comparison that existed between these brothers? We don't know.

Nevertheless, because they were related and they were both in ministry, there was a unique connection between the church in Ephesus and the church in Smyrna. Eventually, Polycarp became the pastor in Smyrna, and it became known as a suffering church.

Pergamum was the next city Jesus sent a message to, and it was the seat of the Roman Proconsul, or governor, over all of Asia. What happened in Pergamum affected the whole continent, so it was vital that a church be there. Thus, this "royal city" as it was known, was also a very important location. It seems that persecution in Asia began in Pergamum, and its shadow eventually fell on the entire region. We know that the first pastor was Antipas, whose name is listed in Revelation 2:13. After Antipas, Early Christian writings tell us the pastor who followed him was named Gaius, and it is likely that Gaius was the pastor when John wrote the book of Revelation.

Then just up the road from Pergamum was the city of **Thyatira**, and it was constructed to protect Pergamum, the treasure city. Thyatira served as a barricade against eastern invaders who might try to attack Pergamum. In this city there was also a significant church.

A few miles away was the city of **Sardis** where the legendary King Croesus lived. He was noted to be the wealthiest man in the world during his time. Croesus ruled the Lydian Kingdom from the capital city of Sardis, and like all the other cities on this circular road, it contained a Christian church.

The fifth city Jesus sent a message to was just up the road from Sardis, and it was the city of **Philadelphia** on the eastern side of Asia. Interestingly, Jesus told the church of Philadelphia, "…I have set before thee an open door…" (Revelation 3:8). The reason this is important is that historically, Philadelphia was the open door, or passageway, to travel to the East. By telling the church in that city, "I have set before you an open door," really meant they were a mission-minded, evangelistic church that had God's favor to take the Gospel further into the East.

The city of **Laodicea** was the last on the circuit, and it was a city of great wealth. Jesus Himself confirmed this in Revelation 3:17, saying they were "rich and increased with goods." When you see the ruins in Laodicea, it's not hard to understand why He made that statement. We know from the calculations done by archaeologists that Laodicea had about 4,500 shops. Indeed, it was a city of opulence with an abundance of commerce.

Jesus Said, 'I Know Thy Works'

Keep in mind, in all seven of these cities there were churches, and all of them had significant, positive aspects about them. At the same time, they each had their own set of challenges and problems. Jesus was very familiar with all these churches. In fact, to all seven of these churches, He said, "I know thy works," and in all seven instances, the word "know" is the Greek word *oida*. This word is from a root that means *to see* or *to make a personal observation*, which means what Jesus knew about these churches was not what someone told Him in prayer. The facts about each church had been personally observed by Jesus Himself. He had been in these churches.

This is made clear in Revelation 2:1, where Jesus said He is the One "...who walketh in the midst of the seven golden candlesticks." The word "midst" here is the word *mesos*, which means *in the very middle* or *in the very center* and depicts *being in the gut or heart of a thing*. Jesus literally walked through the middle of these churches, which is why He could say, "I know (*oida*) thy works."

By using this word *oida*, it is the equivalent of Jesus saying, "I know your works — not because an angel told Me, or someone relayed it to Me in prayer. I know your works because I've seen them with My own eyes as I've walked in the very heart of your church." This brings us to the word "works," which is the Greek word *erga*, and it describes *all of your activities*. Thus, Jesus said, "I personally know everything about you, including all of your activities. There's nothing about you that I do not know."

From the largest to the smallest, Jesus was very familiar with all the activities of these seven churches. Sometimes we think big churches get all the attention, but in this case, we find that every church had been personally observed by Jesus Himself.

What Did Jesus Say to Each Church?

After Jesus walked through the midst of the **church of Ephesus**, the biggest and most influential church, He said, "...Thou hast left thy first love" (Revelation 2:4). He then said, "Remember therefore from whence thou art fallen, and repent..." (Revelation 2:5).

To the **church of Smyrna**, Jesus said, "I know thy works, and tribulation, and poverty...and I know the blasphemy of them which say they are Jews, and are not, but are the synagogue of Satan. Fear none of those things which thou shalt suffer…" (Revelation 2:9,10). For the church of Smyrna, Jesus had no rebuke — just a strong word of encouragement to stay the course of obedience and not to quit.

To the **church of Pergamum**, Jesus said, "But I have a few things against thee, because thou hast there them that hold the doctrine of Balaam, who taught Balac to cast a stumblingblock before the children of Israel, to eat things sacrificed to idols, and to commit fornication" (Revelation 2:14). Basically, Pergamum had a number of doctrinal errors at work in their church, and Jesus told them to, "Repent; or else I will come unto thee quickly, and will fight against them with the sword of my mouth" (Revelation 2:16).

It seems the **church of Thyatira** was also dealing with doctrinal errors. After noting their works of charity, faith, and patience, Jesus expressed His frustration with them because they were allowing a woman called Jezebel to teach and seduce other believers into committing fornication (*see* Revelation 2:20). They were compromising with the world, and Jesus told them to repent.

To the **church of Sardis**, Jesus said, "…I know thy works, that thou hast a name that thou livest, and art dead. Be watchful, and strengthen the things which remain, that are ready to die…" (Revelation 3:1,2). Again, He told them to repent and hold onto the truth they had heard and received (*see* Revelation 3:3).

When Jesus spoke to the **church of Philadelphia**, He didn't have a specific rebuke. Instead, like the church of Smyrna, He spoke a word of encouragement, which included a specific promise that is connected with the end times. Jesus said, "Because thou hast kept the word of my patience, I also will keep thee from the hour of temptation, which shall come upon all the world, to try them that dwell upon the earth" (Revelation 3:10).

Finally, to the **church of Laodicea**, Jesus said, "I know thy works, that thou art neither cold nor hot: I would thou wert cold or hot" (Revelation 3:15). Again, the Greek word for "know" here is *oida*, and the word "works" is the word *erga*. The use of these words is the equivalent of Jesus saying, "I've seen all of your activities personally with my own eyes. There's nothing about you that I do not know. The fact is you're lukewarm, and because you are, I'm going to vomit you out of my mouth." The church of Laodicea was so carnal and worldly that Christ ended up on the outside of the church asking to be readmitted (*see* Revelation 3:20).

John 'Turned' To See Who Was Speaking

After Jesus instructed John to write a message to the seven churches, the Bible says, "And I [John] turned to see the voice that spake with me…" (Revelation 1:12). As we noted in Lesson 3, this word "turned" describes a literal, *physical move*, which means there was a physical dimension to what John experienced. When John heard this voice from behind him, he knew it was the voice of Jesus. So he turned to see the person speaking, but instead of seeing the Jesus he served with in ministry for over three years, he saw Jesus in a way he had never seen Jesus before.

Of course Jesus doesn't change — He's "…the same yesterday, and to day, and for ever" (Hebrews 13:8). But what John saw was a vision of Jesus that had previously been veiled. This sudden unveiling of what was once hidden is called a "revelation" — the Greek word *apokalupsis*. What was revealed about Jesus had always been there, but it couldn't be seen until that moment.

John said, "And I turned to see the voice that spake with me. And being turned, I saw seven golden candlesticks" (Revelation 1:12). So when John turned to see Christ, the first thing he saw was seven golden candlesticks. We know what the candlesticks are because Revelation 1:20 tells us, "…The seven candlesticks which thou sawest are the seven churches." The candlesticks represent the seven major churches in Asia — one in Ephesus, Smyrna, Pergamum, Thyatira, Sardis, Philadelphia, and Laodicea.

The Church of Jesus Christ Is Like an Oil-Burning Lamp

In Greek, the word "candlesticks" is the word *luchnia*, which describes an *oil burning lamp*, not candles like we use today. These oil lamps were carried by hand, positioned on a table or elevated on a stand. Such lamps were fashioned of earthen clay with a reservoir to hold oil and a wick that gave light in darkness once it was lighted. Oil-burning lamps were vital to life because they were the only source of light in darkness.

As we said, no two lamps were exactly alike because they were handmade. These lamps were crafted by Greeks, Romans, and Jews, and were decorated with intricate engravings that reflected the culture. Although some were round and others were pear-shaped, each lamp had the same basic structure, style, and function. All of them had a reservoir to hold oil and a mouth at the front of the lamp that the oil was poured into. A long wick went down into the reservoir of oil and extended out of the lamp's mouth. The wick would become saturated with oil and then set on fire. These First Century lamps could burn for a very long time, giving light in darkness.

Just as no two lamps were exactly alike, no two churches are the same. Yes, they all have the same basic function and structure. We are the house of God, the temple of the Holy Spirit, and we hold the oil of the Spirit. Yet each church is uniquely positioned by God to shine the light of His truth and glory in a specific way. Just as no two lamps in the First Century pointed in the same direction, no two churches are doing exactly the same thing. Each one has its own mission and its own calling.

Furthermore, just as each lamp had a wick that was saturated with oil and then lit on fire to give light to everyone that was in the house, each church is intended to be God's oil lamp in the world. We are to be filled with the precious oil of the Holy Spirit, have a mouth for declaring the Gospel, and when we are saturated with the Holy Spirit and set on fire with the power of God, we become a bright, shining lamp to give light in darkness. That is the purpose of the Church.

In Christ's Eyes, the Church Is Golden

As we saw previously, First Century oil lamps were made of clay, which means they were very fragile, easily breakable, and had noticeable defects. In John's vision, however, he saw seven candlesticks made of *gold*. The word "golden" in Revelation 1:12 is the Greek word *chrusos*, and it describes the *most valuable metal or commodity that existed in the ancient world*. Nothing was more valuable in the First Century than *chrusos* — *pure gold*. The statement being made here by Jesus is that He sees His Church as *pure gold*, not defective clay.

There are people today who can only see the defects in their church. They see all the faults of their pastor as well as the failures of the people they go to church with. Their mind seems to constantly be focused on what their church should be doing and where they are coming up short. The truth is, there is no perfect church. The fact that we are in it makes it imperfect!

The same was true of the seven churches in Asia that Jesus spoke to in Revelation. They all had challenges, yet, even with their defects Jesus still said, "They are golden to Me." Remember, He paid the price to redeem the Church, giving His life's Blood for her. Even though from a human perspective churches have defects, it doesn't matter to Jesus. Each church is a container of the oil of His Spirit, and they are precious to Him. They are gold.

Friend, if this is Jesus' opinion of the Church, then it needs to be *our* opinion of the Church. In spite of its defects and problems, He doesn't shun the Church nor is He ashamed of the Church. And just as He walked up and down in the very center of the seven churches in Asia, He is walking up and down in the heart of every church today. He is proud to be associated with His Church because it is the container of the Holy Spirit, giving light in darkness.

John Saw Jesus As Our High Priest

John continued his description of Jesus by saying, "And in the midst of the seven candlesticks one like unto the Son of man, clothed with a garment down to the foot, and girt about the paps with a golden girdle" (Revelation 1:13). Notice the phrase "like unto." It is a translation of a Greek word that means *to have the resemblance of.* In this case, the person John saw on Patmos *had the resemblance of the Son of man.* That is, He looked like the Jesus that John had known in the flesh, but at the same time, He also looked very different.

Notice the first thing John described about Jesus: "He was clothed with a garment down to the foot." He didn't first talk about His eyes being like a flame of fire or the two-edged sword that came out of His mouth. Instead, the first thing John saw was that He was "clothed with a garment down to the foot."

The reason this phrase is so significant is because it describes the exact clothing of the high priest that is described in Exodus 28. As we read further in chapter 1, we will see that Jesus' feet are uncovered, having no shoes. In fact, John said, "And his feet like unto fine brass..." (Revelation 1:15). In Scripture, brass represents *judgment.* Thus, the indication here is that Jesus is coming with judgment to the churches that would not repent. Yet, before He is seen coming in judgment, He is first and foremost seen as a High Priest standing in the very gut of the Church praying for her.

Hebrews 7:25 tells us that Jesus lives to make intercession for us. That is a picture of what John saw and wrote about in Revelation 1. Even with all the churches' problems and flaws, Jesus continues to stand in the midst of His Church, not shunning us or ashamed of us. Rather, He is praying for these churches to hear His voice and to repent and for them to persevere in their faith as overcomers. What else did John say about Jesus' appearance? We'll look at that in our final lesson.

STUDY QUESTIONS

Study to shew thyself approved unto God, a workman that needeth not to be ashamed, rightly dividing the word of truth.
— 2 Timothy 2:15

1. While it's absolutely important to confront sin in the Church (*see* Matthew 18:15-17; Galatians 6:1-3), it's also crucial to see the Church with Jesus' eyes and to love its members the way He does. What are some practical examples of what this might look like? (*Consider* First Corinthians 13:4-8 and Ephesians 4:1-6,17-32.)

2. Jesus knew that we would need Him as our Advocate and compassionate High Priest (*see* 1 John 2:1; Hebrews 4:15). As He is interceding for each of us in Heaven, who is also interceding for us here on earth? (*See* John 16:7-15 and Romans 8:26,27.)

3. Knowing that God is truly for us, how can we approach Him? (*See* Romans 8:31-34; Hebrews 4:15,16; 10:19-22; and Ephesians 3:12.)

PRACTICAL APPLICATION

But be ye doers of the word, and not hearers only, deceiving your own selves.
— James 1:22

1. It can be so easy to get frustrated by the flaws of your church, your pastor, or even the Church as a whole, but Jesus' heart towards His Church is very different. How have you seen the Church up to now? What offenses tend to keep you from having compassion for other believers?

2. Holding onto offense toward others is deadly. It is one of the primary reasons God's people lack His power, joy, and peace. Pause for a moment and pray: *Holy Spirit, are there people I'm offended with? Has someone in my family, at work, or in the Church disappointed me or hurt me, and I've been unwilling to forgive? Please show me. In Jesus' name.* Whatever names or faces He brings to mind, follow these biblical steps:

- REPENT of holding onto unforgiveness/offense.
- RELEASE the person into God's hands (He is the one and only Judge).
- RECEIVE God's healing power as you invite Him to restore your soul.
- PRAY A BLESSING on those who mistreated you as God says in First Peter 3:8,9.

3. What does it mean to you to know that Jesus is constantly interceding for you? How does it change your view of His heart towards *you*?

LESSON 5

TOPIC

John's Vision of the Exalted Christ

SCRIPTURES

1. **Revelation 1:12-20** — And I turned to see the voice that spake with me. And being turned, I saw seven golden candlesticks; and in the midst of the seven candlesticks one like unto the Son of man, clothed with a garment down to the foot, and girt about the paps with a golden girdle. His head and his hairs were white like wool, as white as snow; and his eyes were as a flame of fire; And his feet like unto fine brass, as if they burned in a furnace; and his voice as the sound of many waters. And he had in his right hand seven stars: and out of his mouth went a sharp twoedged sword: and his countenance was as the sun shineth in his strength. And when I saw him, I fell at his feet as dead. And he laid his right hand upon me, saying unto me, Fear not; I am the first and the last: I am he that liveth, and was dead; and, behold, I am alive for evermore, Amen; and have the keys of hell and of death. Write the things which thou hast seen, and the things which are, and the things which shall be hereafter; The mystery of the seven stars which thou sawest in my right hand, and the seven golden candlesticks. The seven stars are the angels of the seven churches: and the seven candlesticks which thou sawest are the seven churches.

2. **Matthew 17:2** — And was transfigured before them: and his face did shine as the sun, and his raiment was white as the light.
3. **Matthew 28:3** — His countenance was like lightning, and his raiment white as snow.
4. **Revelation 2:21** — And I gave her [Jezebel] space to repent of her fornication; and she repented not.

GREEK WORDS

1. "midst" — μέσος (*mesos*): in the very middle; in the very center; to be in the gut or heart of a thing
2. "fine brass" — χαλκολιβάνῳ (*chalkolibano*): a compound of χαλκός (*chalkos*), meaning brass or bronze, representing judgment, and λίβανος (*libanos*), meaning frankincense, representing prayer; when combined, the new word reveals that although Christ's feet are prepared to move toward judgment, they are doused in intercessory prayer that repentance will occur before He arrives to apply judgment; it is the picture of judgment doused in prayer
3. "angels" — ἄγγελος (*angelos*): messengers, pastors of the seven churches
4. "sword" — ῥομφαία (*rhomphaia*): a very deadly sword

SYNOPSIS

Thus far, we have seen that the apostle John was sent to the isle of Patmos by Emperor Domitian as a political prisoner, and according to Early Christian writers, he was accompanied by his assistant Prochorus, who is mentioned in Acts 6:5 as one of the first deacons of the Church. As a political prisoner, John was allowed to roam the island freely, but he had to find his own food and water. He and his assistant found a cave near the Temple of Artemis where they set up a living space, and it was in that cave that Christ Himself visited John and gave him what we know as the book of Revelation.

On the day when virtually everyone in the Roman Empire was worshiping Emperor Domitian, Jesus stepped into John's cave and began speaking to him, and the Bible says John "…turned to see the voice that spake…" (Revelation 1:12). John knew that voice — how could he forget it? He had heard it nearly every day as he walked side-by-side with Jesus during His earthly ministry. And when he heard that voice, he turned to see the voice that was speaking with him. The word "turned" literally means he *physically turned* to see who was speaking, which indicates there was *a physical element* to the vision John received. The word "spake" here in Greek literally means Jesus was *conversing* with John, and it demonstrates God's desire to carry on conversations with us.

Make no mistake: the Church is precious and priceless to Jesus! And if the Church is precious to Christ, it needs to be precious to us too. In His eyes, we are like *golden* oil-burning lamps that light up the darkness. In spite of our flaws and failures, Christ is not ashamed of us nor does He shun us. Instead, He praises and celebrates our obedience and lovingly corrects us when we are in error. That is what we see Him doing with the seven major churches in Revelation 2 and 3.

As we noted, the churches in Revelation are symbolized as seven golden "candlesticks," which is the Greek word *luchnia*, which describes an *oil burning lamp*. The Bible goes on to say, "And in the midst of the seven candlesticks one like unto the Son of man, clothed with a garment down to the foot, and girt about the paps with a golden girdle" (Revelation 1:13). We've seen that the word "midst" here is the Greek word *mesos*, which means *to be right in the very gut* or *to be right in the very center of something*. The fact that Christ is not on the outside of the Church is important. It tells us He's not shunning the Church — even though He sees its problems, defects, and challenges. Instead, He is proud to be associated with His Church, and it shows because He's walking up and down right in the very heart of it.

The emphasis of this lesson:

John saw Jesus as our Great High Priest, the Emperor of all emperors, the One in control of the universe. His hair and His eyes were beaming the brilliance of God's glory, and His voice was like many waters. Although He does bring correction to the Church, His judgment is slow in coming and doused in prayer. He is the King of kings whose glory is brighter than the noonday sun!

Jesus Is Our High Priest and the Emperor of All Emperors

As we concluded Lesson 4, we noted that the first description John gave of Jesus is that He was "...clothed with a garment down to the foot, and girt about the paps with a golden girdle" (Revelation 1:13). When the Bible says, "Clothed with a garment down to the foot," it means His foot was exposed or uncovered. In other words, Jesus was standing there barefooted, which is exactly the description of the attire of the high priest in Exodus 28. Therefore, before John saw anything else about Jesus, he saw Him first and foremost as the Great High Priest standing in the midst of the troubled church, and as the High Priest, He was making intercession or praying for them. He was praying that they would hear His voice and receive His correction and that they would make it through to the end as overcomers. In the same way, Christ is still praying for the Church today. He's praying that we will hear His voice and receive His correction and walk in obedience. Even with our flaws and mistakes and rebellious moments, He is actively and continually involved in our life. He doesn't shun us or stand there waiting to condemn us when we slip up — He's standing right in the midst of us — His Church.

John goes on to say Jesus was, "…girt about the paps with a golden girdle" (Revelation 1:13). What this means is that around His chest, He had a golden belt, which is important, because kings and emperors at that time wore golden belts. Usually, if they were lowly kings, they wore belts around their waist. The more powerful and wealthy a ruler was, the higher their belt was worn. Thus, a belt worn high around the chest signified this person was quite wealthy. And because the belt was worn so high, it caused their royal robe to move in a majestic sweeping motion. So when we see Christ with a golden belt around His chest, it tells us that He is extremely wealthy, and His robe, which goes down to the foot, is majestically moving as He walks.

It's important to note that even wealthy kings at that time didn't wear belts that were made of solid gold. Yet, that is what Christ was wearing when John saw Him. This Greek word for "girdle" here describes *a very broad belt*, and it was made of solid gold. Very few kings — if any — could afford such a belt. Instead, most kings wore strands of gold that were woven together with other kinds of fabric. The fact that Christ is wearing a belt of solid gold indicates His great power, wealth, and majesty. He doesn't just have strands of gold — He has a wide, solid gold belt wrapped around His chest.

This imagery was important for John to see because he had been exiled by a wicked emperor named Domitian who was ruling in Rome and seemed to have power over all. This solid-gold belt worn across the chest by Christ spoke volumes to John. It said that no one compares to Christ! He is the Emperor of all emperors and supreme in majesty! He is all-sufficient, all-powerful, and fully supplied with all the resources to meet every need we'll ever have.

His Hair and His Eyes
Displayed His Great Glory

John went on to say that Jesus' "…head and his hairs were white like wool, as white as snow…" (Revelation 1:14). Very often, when you see an artist's rendition of this Jesus, they illustrate Him with white hair, but that's not what this verse means. The phrase "white as wool" here is the same phrase used in Matthew 17:2 to describe the shining glory that emanated from Jesus on the Mount of Transfiguration. It's also the exact same word used in Matthew 28:3 to describe the angel's appearance at Jesus' resurrection that was as brilliant as "lightning."

So when the Bible says, "His head and his hairs were white like wool, as white as snow…" (Revelation 1:14), it's really describing *the glory of God* that was beaming from Christ. Imagine it. John saw Jesus as our Great High Priest, the Emperor of all emperors, and now as the radiant glory of God Himself! He was so overwhelmed by this Revelation of Christ that he eventually fell to the ground as a dead man (*see* Revelation 1:17). This is a side of Jesus that John had never seen before.

Then John added, "…And his eyes were as a flame of fire" (Revelation 1:14). Here again, many artists read this and portray Jesus as literally having fire in His eyes, but that is not what the verse says. The key word here is the word *as* — His eyes were "as" a flame of fire." To be *as* a flame of fire means Jesus' eyes had the characteristics of fire. Interestingly, the phrase "flame of fire" here is a translation of the Greek word *phlox*, which describes *a flame of fire that is flickering, swirling, and twirling as it arches and bends upward.*

Have you ever stared at a fire? When you look into the flames, it has a mesmerizing, magnetic pull that draws you in, almost as if it has an intelligence all its own. Sometimes you can nearly get lost looking into a fire because it is so captivating. When John says, "…His eyes were as a flame of fire" (Revelation 1:14), he is telling us that when he looked into the eyes of Jesus he saw intelligence and a magnetism that completely captivated his attention. He had never seen such eyes as the eyes of Jesus. In fact, in the Greek, it actually says, "The eyes of Him were as a flame of fire."

His Feet Were Like 'Fine Brass'

What else did John notice when he saw Jesus? He said, "And his feet were like unto fine brass, as if they burned in a furnace…" (Revelation 1:15). We know from verse 13 that He wore "a garment down to His foot," which indicates His feet were uncovered. Since verse 15 says "His feet," we know it is both feet that appear to be "like unto fine brass, as if they burned in a furnace."

The Greek word here for "fine brass" is very strange. It is a compound of two words: the word *chalkos,* which is the word for *brass* or *bronze,* and represents judgment in Scripture; and the word *libanos,* which is the word for *"frankincense"* and represents *prayer.* Frankincense was the incense, or perfume, that was used by the high priest in the temple — particularly in the Holy of Holies. If you were able to enter into the Holy of Holies like the high priest, you would have smelled the aroma of frankincense, which again was symbolic of prayer.

When we compound the words together *chalkos* and *libanos,* it forms the Greek word *chalkolibano.* The reason this word is strange is because you cannot mix bronze and frankincense. One is a perfume, and the other is an alloy, and the two do not mix. Nevertheless, that is what we find being joined in this text. So what is the Holy Spirit trying to say to us by using this word, *chalkolibano,* to describe the feet of Jesus?

Essentially, He is telling us that Jesus' feet are like *bronze that are doused with frankincense.* The *King James* translators didn't know how to explain this meaning, so they rendered it "feet like unto fine brass, as if they burned in a furnace" (Revelation 1:15). Keep in mind five of the churches that Christ addressed in Revelation 2 and 3 had serious problems, so much so that He commanded them to repent.

In a certain sense, "feet like unto fine brass" indicates that Jesus was coming with judgment to deal with the things that were wrong inside each church. Yet, at the same time, He was not in a rush to judge. His slowness to judge is signified by the fact that His feet are made of brass, and while He is walking in the direction of these churches in order to judge what is wrong, He is moving very slowly.

Friend, Christ is never in a rush to dole out judgment — He always wants to help us repent and come closer to Him. Think about your own life and the things that you've done wrong, the sins that easily trip you up. Hasn't God always given you ample time to repent? Again and again, His Spirit has brought conviction (NOT condemnation) and warned you in advance to self-correct and do what's right. That's what we find Jesus doing with the seven churches He's talking to in the book of Revelation. He's not running to judge them. Instead, He was slowly moving in their direction one foot at a time — praying for them to hear His voice and repent before He arrives with judgment. Again, the word *libanos* is the Greek word for "frankincense." So the picture being painted in Revelation 1:15 is Jesus' *judgment is soaked in prayer*. Christ is interceding for them as a Great High Priest.

Jesus Gave the Church of Thyatira 'Space To Repent'

A perfect example of Jesus being slow to bring judgment is found in His message to the church of Thyatira. After praising them for their works of charity and faith marked by patience, Jesus said, "Notwithstanding I have a few things against thee, because thou sufferest that woman Jezebel, which calleth herself a prophetess, to teach and to seduce my servants to commit fornication, and to eat things sacrificed unto idols " (Revelation 2:20).

Jesus went on to say, "…I gave her space to repent of her fornication; and she repented not" (Revelation 1:21). This tells us plainly that Jesus warned her and gave her time to repent and make things right. He didn't quickly judge her, which is exactly what John was communicating when he said Jesus' "…feet were like unto fine brass, as if they burned in a furnace…" (Revelation 1:15).

Again, Jesus is coming to deal with what is wrong in the Church, but He is moving very slowly (which is symbolized by "brass feet"). As He is walking steadily in our direction to bring judgment (*chalkos*), He is sending a message, telling us what we need to change. At the same time He is praying for us (which is symbolized by frankincense, *libanos*). He is hoping and believing that we'll self-correct, so He doesn't have to appear and deliver judgment.

In fact, John said His feet were like fine brass, "…as if they burned in a furnace…" (Revelation 1:15). The fact that the brass is still in the furnace means it is not hard yet. It is still pliable and has not yet been set. This tells us that although Jesus has to bring correction, that correction is not fixed and set in stone. In other words, these churches still have time to repent and avoid judgment. Praise God for His loving mercy in the way He deals with us!

The Voice of Jesus Is Like 'Many Waters' and He Held Seven Stars in His Hand

In Revelation 1:15, John also tells us Jesus' voice was "…as the sound of many waters." This must have been easy for John to write because he was living on the isle of Patmos with water all around him. From the cave where he and Prochorus were living, he could hear the sounds of the roaring sea, and if there was a storm, the splash of the waves beating against the beach and crashing on the rocks was nearly overwhelming.

Basically, what John is saying is that when Jesus was speaking to him, His voice was so loud and strong it was like the thunderous roar of the sea. No one else could be heard over the sound of His voice because it was so overpowering.

Then when we come to verse 16, John added, "And he had in his right hand seven stars: and out of his mouth went a sharp twoedged sword: and his countenance was as the sun shineth in his strength" (Revelation 1:16).

First of all, notice John says the stars are in Jesus' *right* hand. The right hand always represents a position of authority or power. John said, "And he had in His right hand seven stars…" (Revelation 1:16). The word "had" here is the Greek word *echo*, which means a *firm grip*. These seven stars were in the firm control of Christ, and they have authority and power because they are in His right hand.

What are the seven stars? Revelation 1:20 tells us, "…The seven stars are the angels of the seven churches…." The word "angels" here is the Greek word *angelos*, which means *messengers*. A better translation of this part of the verse would be "the seven messengers" or "the seven pastors of the seven churches."

Thus, Christ has a firm grip on the pastors of these seven major churches in Asia. They are not under the control of the deacon board or the board of directors. They don't even belong to the church. The fact that they are in Christ's right hand means they oversee the church in His authority and power, and they belong to Him and are answerable to Him. Remember, the fivefold ministry gifts are from Christ to the Church, and people in those positions report directly to God for the way they lead others.

An Unfamiliar, Yet Powerful Meaning of the Seven Stars

There is something else that is very important about John's statement, "And he had in his right hand seven stars…" Revelation 1:16). If you remember, John had been exiled by Domitian as a prisoner on Patmos. Domitian had declared that he was god, and when his son died earlier, he had minted a coin with his image on one side and the image of his deceased son on the flip side. Interestingly, Domitian depicted his dead son sitting on a globe of the earth, playing with seven stars, and the dead child was portrayed as the god Zeus or Jupiter.

By minting this coin, Domitian was saying, "My dead child is now deified. He is as great as the gods Zeus and Jupiter, and he's so great he's playing with the seven stars of the universe." Furthermore, by minting this coin and proclaiming that his child was like Jupiter or Zeus, Domitian was saying, "If my child is god, who do you think I am? I'm greater than God Himself. In fact, I'm the greatest of all gods." This coin depicting Domitian and Domitian's son playing with the seven stars was his way of saying, "I have authority even over the universe."

So when Jesus appears before John with seven stars in His right hand, He is declaring, "Hey John, look what I have in my hand. I'm the One with the seven stars! If you want to know who is King of kings and the Lord of the universe, look no further. It is not demented Domitian who is sitting on the throne in Rome and who exiled you to this island. It's Me!" Thus, John's vision of Jesus holding the seven stars in His right hand is Jesus' declaration of His supreme deity.

A Two-Edged Sword Extends From Jesus' Mouth

John goes on to say, "…And out of his mouth went a sharp twoedged sword…" (Revelation 1:16). The word "sword" here is the Greek word *rhomphaia*, which describes *a very deadly sword*. In this verse, Christ is portrayed as coming with a sword to eradicate the spiritual disease that was trying to invade the churches.

We know from Revelation 2 that the church of Ephesus and the church of Pergamum were dealing with the doctrine of the Nicolaitans, which was a deadly teaching of compromise that was neutralizing the efforts of the laypeople in the Church. Although Jesus didn't hate the Nicolaitans, He did hate their teaching and their works. In a similar way, the Bible reveals that the church of Thyatira also had been seduced by false doctrine. Jesus loved these churches so much that He didn't ignore their problems, but rather, He lovingly corrected them.

Still today, Christ loves the Church, and from time to time, He will do what is necessary to confront our compromise and remove the ungodly elements that need to be removed. And that's what we now find happening in these verses.

Christ's Glory Is Extraordinarily Brilliant

Then John said, "…And his countenance was as the sun shineth in his strength" (Revelation 1:16). Here we have a picture of glory so brilliant you can hardly bear to look at it. The phrase "as the sun shineth in his strength" is a picture of a person looking directly into the sun at the most intense moment of the day.

What's interesting is that the same Greek word used here is also used to describe what happens in the winter when the sun is out in all of its glory, and it shines on the glistening snow. Indeed, the reflection of its rays becomes a blinding light that is extremely difficult to look at because it is so glorious. Basically, what John is saying is, "Looking at Jesus was like trying to stare directly into the sun at the most intense time of the day. His glory was so great I could hardly look at Him."

Are you seeing the intensity of John's Revelation of Jesus? He appears as…

- Our Great High Priest (Revelation 1:13).
- The Emperor of all emperors (Revelation 1:14).
- The radiant glory of God with eyes as fire (Revelation 1:14).
- The Judge who is slowly coming, praying for His Church to repent (Revelation 1:15).
- The voice that sounds like many waters (Revelation 1:15).
- The One who controls the universe (Revelation 1:16).
- The sun shining in all of its strength (Revelation 1:16).

How did John respond when he saw all of these attributes? John said, "And when I saw him, I fell at his feet as dead. And he laid his right hand upon me, saying unto me, Fear not; I am the first and the last: I am he that liveth, and was dead; and, behold, I am alive for evermore, Amen; and have the keys of hell and of death. Write the things which thou hast seen, and the things which are, and the things which shall be hereafter" (Revelation 1:17-19).

Wow! Who is like Jesus Christ? He is the Alpha and Omega, the Beginning and the End, and everything in between. He is worthy of all praise, all glory, and all honor. Let us worship Him with our very lives and be busy about His business — shining the light of truth to those in darkness. And may we be ready for His soon return!

STUDY QUESTIONS

Study to shew thyself approved unto God, a workman that needeth not to be ashamed, rightly dividing the word of truth.
— 2 Timothy 2:15

1. Jesus is not only interceding for us as the Church, but He's standing right in the center of the Church as He prays for us, proving that He's not put off by our challenges, struggles, or mistakes. Instead, He's intimately, actively involved in our lives at every moment. What else does Scripture say about how close Jesus is to us? (*Read* Psalm 34:18; 145:18; James 4:8; and Acts 17:27.)

2. Knowing that Jesus is our Judge as well as our High Priest, we can see that He is responsible to bring judgment at times, yet His heart is always to show mercy and help us get back on track (i.e. His judgment is always slow and doused in prayer). What does God want us to do so that He doesn't have to deliver judgment in our lives? (*Consider* Lamentations 3:40,41; First Corinthians 11:31,32; Second Corinthians 13:5; and First John 3:18-21.)

PRACTICAL APPLICATION

But be ye doers of the word, and not hearers only, deceiving your own selves.
— James 1:22

1. Has anything happened in your life to make you feel as though Jesus is far from you? If so, what was it? How does it feel to know that He isn't far removed from you, but right in the middle of your challenges, guiding you with His Spirit and interceding for you before God the Father? Take a few minutes to really let that sink in and journal anything He tells or shows you.

2. One of many ways Jesus shows His love for us is through lovingly correcting us when we start to stray off the path — kind of like a good shepherd would nudge his sheep away from a cliff. In what areas has the Lord been bringing correction to your life? How does Hebrews 12:5-11 help you see and receive His discipline rather than resist it?

3. In order for us to experience the benefits of His conviction, we need to repent, or turn around and cooperate with Him as He's redirecting us. What is His response when we do this? (*See* Second Chronicles 7:14; First John 1:9; Acts 3:19; Proverbs 28:13; Joel 2:12,13; and Ezekiel 18:32.)

A Prayer To Receive Salvation

If you've never received Jesus as your Savior and Lord, now is the time for you to experience the new life Jesus wants to give you! To receive God's gift of salvation that can be obtained through Jesus alone, pray this prayer from your heart:

> *Jesus, I repent of my sin and receive You as my Savior and Lord. Wash away my sin with Your precious blood and make me completely new. I thank You that my sin is removed, and Satan no longer has any right to lay claim on me. Through Your empowering grace, I faithfully promise that I will serve You as my Lord for the rest of my life.*

If you just prayed this prayer of salvation, you are born again! You are a brand-new creation in Christ! Would you please let us know of your decision by going to **renner.org/salvation**? We would love to connect with you and pray for you as you begin your new life in Christ.

Scriptures for further study: John 3:16; John 14:6; Acts 4:12; Ephesians 1:7; Hebrews 10:19,20; 1 Peter 1:18,19; Romans 10:9,10; Colossians 1:13; 2 Corinthians 5:17; Romans 6:4; 1 Peter 1:3

Notes

Notes

CLAIM YOUR FREE RESOURCE!

As a way of introducing you further to the teaching ministry of Rick Renner, we would like to send you FREE of charge his teaching, "How To Receive a Miraculous Touch From God" on CD or as an MP3 download.

In His earthly ministry, Jesus commonly healed *all* who were sick of *all* their diseases. In this profound message, learn about the manifold dimensions of Christ's wisdom, goodness, power, and love toward all humanity who came to Him in faith with their needs.

☑ **YES, I want to receive Rick Renner's monthly teaching letter!**

Simply scan the QR code to claim this resource or go to: **renner.org/claim-your-free-offer**

Connect

WITH US!

www.ingramcontent.com/pod-product-compliance
Lightning Source LLC
Chambersburg PA
CBHW071642040426
42452CB00009B/1733